**Genre** Expository

**Essential Question**
How do natural events a
affect the environment?

M000192045

# The Great Plains

BY KEN BENN

The Great Plains of North America, also known as the Prairies, span an area of half a million square miles. This immense region of grassland reaches beyond the United States border into Canada in the north. To the south, it stretches all the way through Texas into Mexico. The Rocky Mountains form a distinct border to the west. The eastern border is less clearly defined, although most people say that the Missouri, Arkansas, and Mississippi rivers make a good boundary for the eastern flank.

## THE GREAT PLAINS

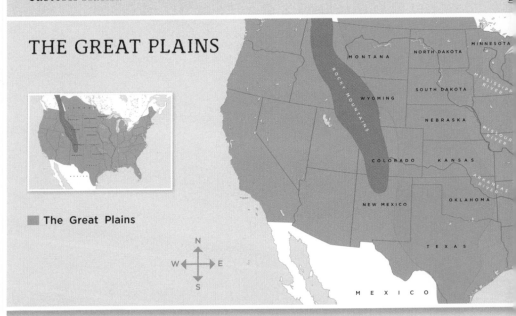

The Great Plains

Scientists think that these vast plains were once under water. The American continent began to uplift about 70 million years ago. The Great Plains developed a diverse range of ecosystems as the water drained from the land. Many different plant and animal **species** thrived in these ecosystems.

Scientists have collected a range of fossils and geological evidence from the Great Plains over the years. This evidence suggests that the region has experienced widespread changes, affecting all its ecosystems to varying extents.

Many natural events, such as droughts, blizzards, and wildfires, have repeatedly challenged the ecosystems. Then, European settlers arrived, and the **ecology** of the Great Plains had to cope with another range of threats.

The early settlers converted large areas of prairie grass for agricultural purposes. They needed land to graze their cattle and sheep, and they planted wheat and other crops, including sorghum, cotton, and flax. The settlers also hunted some species of animals to near extinction.

Many **conservationists** and government agencies would like to restore the ecology of the Great Plains. However, this is no simple task. The first step of its successful restoration is to understand the natural processes of this unique area.

The Great Plains extend over large areas of 11 states.

# CHAPTER 1

# Shaping the Great Plains

Scientists believe that shallow seas covered most of the Great Plains about 70 million years ago. Layers of thick, rich sediment built up on the seafloor. Then, underground forces caused the land to slowly lift, and the waters receded. The Rocky Mountains were pushed up and volcanoes appeared.

Many geological forces continued to shape this new land. Streams carried sediment down from the volcanoes and the Rocky Mountains onto the plains. Mounds of rock and soil built up, and the streams and rivers had to find new paths to reach the oceans. Sometimes the water cut into rock, gouging out canyons and wearing down hills.

Sixty-foot-high sculptures of the faces of presidents George Washington, Thomas Jefferson, Theodore Roosevelt, and Abraham Lincoln are carved into Mount Rushmore in the Black Hills.

Weather and other natural forces shaped the Great Plains into a range of different landforms. For example, the Black Hills are different from the High Plains, and the High Plains are different again from Caprock Canyon. Different ecosystems developed in each area, and this resulted in great **biodiversity** across the Great Plains.

Centuries ago, the land included many freshwater lakes and made the Great Plains the ideal home for numerous large animals, or megafauna. Some of these included the mammoth, a species of camel, the large-headed llama, an ancient species of bison, and the giant predator, the short-faced bear. Now, thousands of years later, all of these animals are **extinct**, and a wide variety of new species inhabit the Great Plains.

## THE BLACK HILLS

The Black Hills are located in southwestern South Dakota and northeastern Wyoming. The peaks in the central part of the Black Hills tower about 3,000 to 4,000 feet above the surrounding plains.

Huge underground pressure lifted the area up. The soft surface sediment then eroded away to expose hard metamorphic rock.

From 1927 to 1941, a group of artists under the guidance of Gutzon Borglum sculpted the faces of four presidents of the United States at Mount Rushmore National Memorial in the Black Hills. Today millions of people from all around the world visit the memorial every year.

Scientists have studied geological records. The records show that the Great Plains have experienced large changes in climate over the ages. There was more rain during the Ice Age, and the overall temperature was cooler. The difference in temperature between summer and winter was not as big as it is today. The plentiful water supply contributed to ideal conditions for lush forests of pine, oak, and juniper to cover much of the region.

At the end of the Ice Age, though, the climate changed. The Great Plains became warmer, and the ice caps receded. The area had to rely on westerly winds to bring moisture from the Pacific Ocean once the ice had gone. However, the Rocky Mountains acted as a barrier, preventing moisture from crossing to the plains, and the Great Plains began to dry out.

The region's vegetation changed from forests to hardier grasslands. Many large animals, such as the mammoth, could not adapt to the changing conditions and died out. Meanwhile, bison adapted and flourished.

By examining fossils and bones, paleontologists find out about animals that once lived on the Great Plains.

The Great Plains have experienced many droughts over the centuries. Droughts affect the ecosystems around streams and other waterways.

The fish in a stream can often escape to other areas when the stream begins to dry up. However, frogs and **crustaceans**, such as shrimp, crabs, and lobsters, are not as mobile as fish, so it is not as easy for them to leave. If the water level drops too low for too long, it is probable that these types of creatures will die. When a stream is drying up, the entire food web along that stream is affected. Even birds and larger animals, such as beavers and raccoons, may be forced to leave the area.

## THE PLIGHT OF THE MUSSEL

Freshwater mussels are important members of the waterway ecosystems of the Great Plains. Mussels are filter feeders, which means that they help keep the water clean, and they are an important part of the food web, too. They provide **protein** for a variety of animals, including fish, rats, raccoons, and birds such as the great blue heron. When a waterway is disrupted, mussel beds can be destroyed, with the mussels being washed away or left high and dry.

Floods, droughts, dams, and humans excavating for gravel can disrupt the flow in a waterway. This can cause problems for the mussels that live there.

# CHAPTER 2

# The Humans Arrive

No one knows for certain when the first humans came to the Great Plains. Scientists have studied bones from an extinct Ice Age camel and two mammoths found on the Great Plains. The way the bones were broken and a piece of rock found with the bones suggest that humans had killed the animals. The bones have been dated as being over 12,000 years old.

Scientists are certain that around 10,000 years ago, the first Native Americans made their homes on the Great Plains. The early residents were mostly **nomadic** people. They followed bison across the grasslands, hunting them and other animals. Native Americans also raised crops such as corn on the Great Plains. They needed space for their vegetables to grow, and they used fire to clear the natural grasses and shrubs from the land. However, overall, they had little impact on the natural environment.

Stone spear heads are among the oldest tools found in North America. The points were tied to the tips of long spears used for hunting megafauna.

(t) Tetra Images/Tetra Images/CORBIS, (b) Oleksiy Maksymenko/Getty Images

In the early sixteenth century, Spanish explorers reached the Great Plains. They traveled on horseback, searching for cities of gold that they believed existed. Their first contact was with the Wichita people near what is now Kansas. The Native Americans had never seen horses before. They quickly recognized the animals' value and were eager to trade for them.

Horses changed the Native Americans' hunting methods. They had hunted in teams on foot, but once they had horses, they could move faster, travel further, and kill more bison.

A hunter on horseback could move as fast as a bison could run.

European fur trappers arrived nearly one hundred years after the Spanish explorers first set foot on the Great Plains. There was a big demand for people to hunt animals for their skins. Felt hats made from beaver skin started the fashion trend of fur caps, gloves, and muffs. There were no laws in place to protect the animals in those days. As a result, the numbers of some animal species, such as the beaver, declined drastically.

Settlers from the United States, or pioneers, began establishing farms on the Great Plains during the nineteenth century. The Homestead Act of 1862 allowed a settler to own up to 160 acres of land. The settlers had to live on the land for five years, and they had to improve the land.

Settlers plowed up large areas of the prairie grasslands to make way for their crops, and this created disorder for the local ecology. The roots of the grasses had been important in holding soil in place and helping reduce soil erosion. The grasslands had also provided a **habitat** for many birds and other animals.

## OGALLALA AQUIFER

The Ogallala Aquifer is a huge supply of water that lies beneath the Great Plains. This water is held between layers of rock. The aquifer extends for approximately 225,000 square miles (580,000 square kilometers).

However, supplies of underground water take a long time to accumulate. They rely on water seeping down from the surface of the land. Currently, people are taking water from the Ogallala Aquifer faster than water is able to flow back in and refill it. Scientists think that it could take 6,000 years for the aquifer to refill naturally once it has been drained.

Water from the Ogallala Aquifer is used to irrigate nearly one-fifth of the wheat, corn, cotton, and cattle farms in the United States.

©Royalty-Free/Corbis

The pioneer farmers tilled the land ceaselessly. They were eager to increase their crop production, and they wanted to graze more livestock. Most of the soil's natural nutrients had been lost by the 1930s.

The farmers started to spread fertilizers over the land to make their crops and pastures grow faster, and they used pesticides, or toxic sprays, to stop insects from eating their crops. The chemicals in the fertilizers and sprays didn't just kill insect pests. They also killed beneficial insects that were an important part of the food webs of the Great Plains.

A series of terrible droughts hit the Great Plains in the 1930s. Crops had replaced much of the hardy prairie grassland. These crops died during the drought. There was nothing left to hold the soil in place. High winds lifted the soil and carried it across the country in thick clouds of dust. In May 1934, a particularly bad storm spread dust from Texas all the way to New York City. People call this period the Dust Bowl.

By the end of 1934, about 100 million acres of topsoil had been lost from farmland, and over three-quarters of the country had been affected.

NOAA George E. Marsh Album

More recently, some farmers have recognized that using more and more fertilizers and pesticides can cause problems, so they have been planting crops such as grain, sorghum, and sunflowers that have been **crossbred** with prairie grasses.

Prairie grasses thrive in the natural conditions of the Great Plains. They don't need chemicals to help them grow well because they have adapted over thousands of years to the conditions in their environment.

These new crops don't need a lot of fertilizers and pesticides, and they are perennial. This means that they will regrow when they have been harvested. These crops are better for the natural ecosystems of the Great Plains. They have very deep roots, and they help prevent soil erosion.

## HUMAN IMPACT ON THE GREAT PLAINS

| DATE | PEOPLE | ACTIVITY | EFFECT |
|------|--------|----------|--------|
| Around 10,000 years ago | First Native Americans | • Cleared small areas for growing vegetables <br> • Hunted bison on foot | • Burned some areas of natural vegetation <br> • Killed some bison |
| Early 16th century | Spanish explorers | • Introduced horses | • Many more bison killed |
| 16th–19th century | European fur trappers | • Hunted animals for skins and pelts | • Many animal species declined rapidly, some nearly dying out |
| 19th–20th century | Settlers from the United States | • Plowed up large areas of grassland <br> • Grazed a lot of livestock <br> • Used fertilizers and toxic sprays | • Unstable soil <br> • Nutrients lost <br> • Insects killed, affecting other animals in food web |

# CHAPTER 3

# Rebuilding the Great Plains' Ecosystems

Conservationists are trying to figure out how to help restore the Great Plains. Many conservationists think that we need to start by looking at the prairie grasses. The prairie grasses are the basis for many of the complex food webs in the Great Plains' ecosystems.

Conservationists still have a lot to learn about how these ecosystems are linked throughout the Great Plains. Natural events such as lightning strikes can easily start fires in the dry grasses of the Prairie. At one time, the fires were seen as something bad, and people used to put them out as quickly as possible. However, research has shown that the fires actually help the ecology of the area in a variety of ways. The fires move quickly over the land, burning only the surface of the ground. They help clear away old growth, add nutrients to the soil, and keep pest plants from invading the plains. Many people have changed their thinking as a result of the research about fires.

Prairie plant roots can reach much farther underground than the part of the plant growing above the ground, which helps to protect the plant from fire.

# THE BLACK-FOOTED FERRET AND THE PRAIRIE DOG

The black-footed ferret is one of the most endangered animals in North America. One of the reasons is that the population of its main food source, the prairie dog, has drastically declined.

Prairie dogs are a type of squirrel. They range throughout much of the Great Plains. Prairie dogs play an important role in the ecology of the Great Plains. They eat grasses and turn the soil as they burrow. This helps encourage grasses to grow and helps water filter through the soil. Prairie dog burrows also help channel water into underground aquifers.

However, many farmers don't like prairie dogs. They want the grass to be left for their livestock to eat. People and animals such as horses and cattle can trip in the prairie dogs' burrows and injure themselves. For this reason, most farmers think that the prairie dog is a pest.

Conservationists are also developing projects to help protect and increase the populations of bison, black-footed ferrets, prairie dogs, and wolves that once roamed freely across the Great Plains. Restoring an animal population can be a challenge. First, conservationists need to ensure that there is an adequate supply of the main food of the species available.

In 1987, conservationists captured 18 wild black-footed ferrets and began a recovery program, but the ferret will probably not survive unless the prairie dog (below) is saved.

Conservationists are also learning about the bison's role in the prairie's ecological system. Bison help keep the prairie healthy. They spread prairie grass seeds, fertilize the ground, and keep the grass short with their grazing. This benefits prairie dogs because these rodents only eat short grass.

Scientists believe that at least 30 million bison once roamed the Great Plains. Today there are only a few small wild herds, with the largest herds found in Yellowstone National Park and Wood Buffalo National Park in Canada.

Some conservationists want to restore bison across the Great Plains. However, they face obstacles. In the past, some bison crossbred with domestic cattle. Now it can be hard to identify the purebred bison.

Also, some farmers are worried because some bison might carry a disease. The farmers fear that the diseased bison might infect their cattle. Conservationists will need to convince the farmers to support their plans for restoring the bison to the Great Plains.

There are approximately 500,000 bison in North America today, with most of these living in national parks or wildlife areas.

# Conclusion

The Great Plains formed slowly over tens of millions of years. Movements deep inside Earth pushed up the land and forced the seas to drain. The weather played a part, too. Now the Great Plains are home to a large variety of **interconnected** ecosystems.

Many of the Great Plains' ecosystems have changed over time. Climate change, droughts, fires, storms, and human activity have all left their mark on the Great Plains.

Many of the animal species that made their homes on the Great Plains have faced pressures on their natural habitats or their sources of food. Some of these animals have become extinct. Others are threatened with extinction.

Even plants of the Great Plains, such as the prairie grasses, have faced challenges. Some people think that we can only protect the Great Plains by first restoring the grasslands. After all, the prairie grasses are the foundation for the many complex food webs of the Great Plains.

However, restoring the ecology of the Great Plains is a complicated task. All the ecosystems are closely linked. This can make it difficult to figure out which specific animal or plant species should be restored first.

We need to conduct more research to help us better understand the biodiversity of the Great Plains. A greater understanding will ensure that we are more careful about how we restore this important region. Also, the people who live on the Great Plains need to be encouraged to get involved, and they need to be educated about the ecological issues of the area so that they can understand why it is so important to protect the unique environment that is their home.

# Respond to Reading

## Summarize

Use the most important details from *The Great Plains* to summarize the selection. Your graphic organizer may help you.

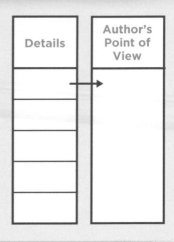

| Details | Author's Point of View |
|---------|------------------------|
|         |                        |
|         |                        |
|         |                        |
|         |                        |

## Text Evidence

**1.** What features of *The Great Plains* help you identify it as expository text? **GENRE**

**2.** What is the author's point of view about the Great Plains? What evidence does the author include to support this position? **AUTHOR'S POINT OF VIEW**

**3.** The word *toxic* on page 11 contains the root *tox*, meaning "poison." Use the root word and context clues to define the word *toxic*. **ROOT WORDS**

**4.** What is the author's point of view about the human impact on the Great Plains in Chapter 2? Write about how details from the text communicate this point of view. **WRITE ABOUT READING**

## Compare Texts

Read about the return of wolves to the Great Plains.

# Save the Great Plains Wolves

The beautiful Great Plains wolf once roamed far and wide across the Great Plains. However, many farmers and hunters did not like these remarkable creatures. The farmers said that wolves attacked their cattle, and the hunters said the wolves competed with hunters for the deer and elk that the hunters enjoyed tracking. Both farmers and hunters argued that the wolves were pests. People decided to track and poison the wolves to get rid of them. The wolves were defenseless against the unexpected attacks. Before long, the wolves had been hunted and killed until they were nearly extinct.

Scientists have observed wolves carefully, and they have made some amazing discoveries. It is important that we act to save the Great Plains wolf for several reasons.

The Great Plains wolf once ranged throughout the United States and southern Canada.

Alan Carey/CORBIS

First, Great Plains wolves, also known as buffalo wolves, are important members of the Great Plains' ecosystems. Scientists have discovered that deer and elk herds get too big when there are no wolves hunting them. It is difficult for large herds to find enough food. Wolves help keep deer and elk populations at manageable sizes.

Also, when there are no wolves around, the deer and elk herds will camp in one place over winter instead of moving around. They will graze on the same young trees until all the tender branches and leaves have been eaten away, and the trees cannot grow anymore.

Wolves encourage deer and elk to move around by their very presence. This gives the trees a chance to grow, which helps the whole ecosystem. Birds and insects live in the trees. Birds feed on the insects. Beavers build their dams from tree branches. The whole environment benefits from the deer and elk moving regularly.

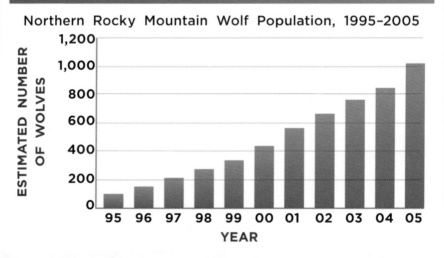

**Reintroducing Wolves**

Wolves have been reintroduced in other parts of the United States. The northern Rocky Mountain wolf was successfully reintroduced in the Yellowstone area in 1995.

Northern Rocky Mountain Wolf Population, 1995–2005

Second, wolves might not be a problem for farmers. Scientists have discovered that wolves pick out weak or sick animals when they hunt. If cattle ranchers look after their cattle, wolves will not hunt them. In fact, people have seen wolves walk right through a herd of cattle without touching a single one in order to hunt a deer on the other side of the paddock!

Third, wolves could help people earn money. These incredible creatures are a great tourist attraction, and tourists will spend money to see Great Plains wolves in their natural habitat.

Humans almost wiped out the Great Plains wolves once. This had the effect of placing other plants and animals of the plains' ecosystems at risk. Now we understand how important it is to save the wolves. Saving the wolves will help save the Great Plains!

Farmers can help save the Great Plains wolf by taking good care of cattle.

William Campbell/CORBIS

## Make Connections

What have scientists learned about the role of wolves on the Great Plains? **ESSENTIAL QUESTION**

What do wolves and prairie dogs have in common? How are they both important to the Great Plains? **TEXT TO TEXT**

# Glossary

**biodiversity** *(bigh-oh-di-VUR-si-tee)* many different types of plants and animals in an area *(page 5)*

**conservationists** *(kon-suhr-VAY-shuh-nists)* people who want to protect things, especially natural things in the environment such as animals and plants *(page 3)*

**crossbred** *(KRAWS-bred)* crossed two different breeds of an animal or a plant to produce an animal or plant that is a mixed breed *(page 12)*

**crustaceans** *(kru-STAY-shuhnz)* animals that mainly live in water and have hard shells, two antennae, and no backbone; for example, lobsters, crabs, shrimp, and barnacles *(page 7)*

**ecology** *(ee-KOL-uh-jee)* an area of science that looks at how living things relate to their environment *(page 3)*

**extinct** *(ek-STINGKT)* describes a plant or animal that is no longer alive on Earth *(page 5)*

**habitat** *(HAB-i-tat)* the natural environment of a living thing *(page 10)*

**interconnected** *(in-tuhr-kuh-NEK-tid)* joined or related in some way *(page 16)*

**nomadic** *(noh-MAD-ik)* moving from place to place *(page 8)*

**protein** *(PROH-teen)* a rich food that is found in plants and animals and is a necessary part of every animal's diet *(page 7)*

**species** *(SPEE-sheez)* a group of plants or animals that share the same features, come from the same family, and are able to breed together *(page 2)*

# Index

**Focus on Science**

**Purpose** To understand the impact that the extinction of an animal has on the environment

## Procedure

**Step 1** With a partner or a group, choose one Great Plains animal that you'd like to learn more about.

**Step 2** Research the animal. Identify its role in the ecosystem. Think about what would happen if the animal became extinct. How would the food web be affected? How would the environment it lives in be affected?

**Step 3** Make a list of arguments for and against protecting your animal. You will need to be able to convince your classmates how important your animal is. In order to defend it, you will also need to know why someone would say that your animal isn't worth saving.

**Step 4** Set up a class debate in which each pair or group argues for its animal. Have the class vote at the end of the debate on which animal to protect.

**Conclusion** Which kinds of animals are the easiest to defend? Is it possible for humans to live in harmony with the animal you researched? Why or why not?

Made in the USA
Coppell, TX
19 June 2023

18297418R00039

- Active vs. passive voice
- Showing vs. telling
- Grammar
- Punctuation
- Dialogue, and more.

An edit contributes to the smooth flow of your story and makes writing tight by deleting what's unnecessary.

"But I can't afford a professional editor," you say.

You can't afford not to hire one. The quality — or lack thereof — of your story directly impacts your sales. And who doesn't want lots of sales?

I don't say this just because I'm a freelance editor. Even editors need their work edited. That's because it's hard for us see what's wrong with our own writing. You might catch some of those typos and punctuation errors, but when it comes to big issues like plot and character development, we can miss the mark. *That's* why I encourage you to hire an editor.

My question to you is, "Are you assuming an editor is horrendously expensive or do you know what those costs really are?"

If not, here are the industry standard fees as listed in *Writer's Market 2021…*

### Rates for fiction content editing (big picture issues)

| **High** | **Low** | **AVG** |
|---|---|---|
| $200/hr | $10/hr | $47/hr |
| $10,000/project | $250/project | $2,428/project |
| 10¢/word | 3¢/word | 5¢/word |
| $25/page | $7/page | $14/page |

DEBRA L. BUTTERFIELD

**Rates for copy editing (mechanics)**

| **High** | **Low** | **AVG** |
|---|---|---|
| $200/hr | $10/hr | $51/hr |
| $3,500/project | $100/project | $1,303/project |
| 14¢/word | 12¢/word | 12¢/word |

Admittedly, I struggle with these rates, so I'm sure you do too. The per hour averages are okay. But there are things we don't know about these figures:

- How many hours did the editor spend doing the job?
- What was the manuscript's average word count?
- How well or poorly written was the manuscript?
- Does this include an additional round of editing?

Rates vary tremendously, which makes it very difficult to know what's a good price and what is a high price. You'll find rates that are per word, per 1000 words, per hour, per page, per project. There's no doubt about it, editing represents the biggest investment you'll make in your book.

Editing isn't a speed read. Stop and think about how long it took you to write your book. It wasn't accomplished in an hour or a day. How many hours does it take you to read your favorite fiction or nonfiction book?

Reading and editing a book takes time, anywhere from ten to over forty hours, depending on the total word count and the type of edit you've requested. The editor is making notes on structure, flow, grammar and punctuation, POV, plot and character development, and a whole lot more.

So let's crunch some numbers. A big-picture edit for a fic-

tion book of 90,000 words could take forty hours (or more). At an hourly rate of $47, that would cost $1,880. At a rate of $0.05/word, that same edit would cost $4,500. In actuality, the hourly rate isn't so bad.

The difficulty for the editor comes in estimating how many hours a job will take. A look at the first chapter isn't always a good guide. Many writers polish the first three chapters because those are what get submitted to acquisition editors. An editor might look at chapter one and estimate ten hours for the whole project, but then find the story falls apart after chapter three, and the job takes two or three times longer to complete.

Unless you write children's books, plan on a *minimum* of twenty hours for an editor to copy edit a book of 70,000 words or more. Developmental edits take longer.

I hope that helps put the cost of editing into a better perspective for you. Yes, editing can be expensive. Shop around and get recommendations from other writers. Begin saving for your editing costs as soon as you start your draft!

Remember, the editing process is designed to make your book baby ready to face the world of readers, aka book buyers — buyers who leap onto Amazon to boo or praise your work. If you have more negative reviews than positive, sales will plummet.

I put together this booklet to help you understand the editing process and its cost, and to show you what you can do to save money. Each cheat sheet is designed to help you fix common errors and refine your writing. After all, the less your editor has to fix, the less time he or she spends on your manuscript. That translates to money saved on your end.

So take a deep breath, relax your jaw, and tell yourself "I'm not in trouble with the principal."

Good. Now, let's take a deeper look at the procedure.

# What Is an Editor's Job?

The primary work of the editor is to make your fiction, or nonfiction, the best it can be. Some editors come across harsh in how they say things. Some are careful not to trample all over the writer — and some don't seem to care. By and large, I believe most try not to wound you. Constructive criticism and rejection are a normal part of publishing. Learn to handle it if you plan to make writing a career.

If you're submitting magazine articles, magazine staff ensure your article is well-developed and fits the tone and style of the magazine (I hope you spent time studying the magazine). In a book, editors look for the elements of plot and character development, active voice, showing, no head hopping, and more. They want chapter openings that hook the reader and chapter endings that spur the reader to turn the page. In nonfiction, they examine structure, organization, and flow. In all books, correct grammar and mechanics are reviewed.

Your work, whether an article or book, will also be edited for style such as that laid out in the *Chicago Manual of Style* and the *Associated Press Stylebook* (AP). The publishing industry tends to use the *Chicago* manual, and magazines and newspapers use AP. Don't get hung up on learning the rules presented in these manuals. Instead, concentrate on writing a great book and you'll likely see less red on the manuscript.

There are different kinds of edits, and from person to person, they may be called by different names. What I call a concept edit others call a big-picture edit. Therefore, when working with a freelancer, it's important to clearly state your expectations and make sure you're both clear on the terminology used. Are you interested in knowing whether your grammar is correct? That requires a copy edit. Do you want to know if your plot and

characters are well-developed? Is the dialogue real, is the pacing off, is the character arc missing? That's a big-picture edit. (See "What Rates the Red Pen?" for more on types of edits.)

You can have as much or as little as you want done in an edit by a freelancer. Which is why you want to be specific and have a conversation before you hire one.

You won't have that kind of control with a traditional publishing house. And no matter how well written, your manuscript will go through some level of editing after it's accepted. They'll provide a report or have a conversation with you to discuss big picture issues you need to fix. They'll fix grammar and mechanics and line edit after you've done big-picture revisions. Don't be afraid to ask who your editor is and what you can expect from him or her. Realize that the more well written your manuscript is, the more you improve the chances it will be accepted.

> No matter how well written, your manuscript will go through some level of editing after it's accepted.

The freelancer is working for you, to improve your book. The traditional publishing house's primary concern is whether the book will be profitable for them (they wouldn't have accepted it if they thought otherwise). The more time a publisher has to spend making your book ready for readers, the lower their profit. In the end, both freelancers and traditional publishers work to make your book the best it can be.

## What Rates the Red Pen?

It really is no wonder that the editing process confuses writers. There are many kinds of edits and the names vary from editor to editor. In my research, I have found little consistency in terminology and what elements were examined. What one calls a macro edit another may call developmental edit. This confusion applies to working with freelancers, not publishers.

The Big Picture Edit, also called a Developmental or Substantive Edit, looks at big-picture aspects. In fiction, that means plot and character development, dialogue, point of view (POV), show vs. tell, active vs. passive voice, pacing, character arc, and more. In nonfiction, it's structure, flow, organization, clarity and relevance of examples/anecdotes, pace, active vs. passive voice, and more. This type of edit involves reading the entire manuscript. The editor then provides a report outlining what is and isn't working, strengths and weaknesses of the manuscript as well as your writing. This report also suggests possible solutions.

A Line or Stylistic Edit, requires working through your manuscript line by line, making edits and entering comments directly in your manuscript. This edit doesn't address big-picture issues, but involves flow and clarity. Sentence elements may get rearranged or whole sentences and paragraphs moved around. The editor will look for vocabulary inappropriate for the audience, too many adjectives/adverbs, transitions, and may even sug-

> Sentence elements may get rearranged or whole sentences and paragraphs moved around.

gest reordering chapters (especially in nonfiction). He then sends the marked manuscript back to you to review and revise.

The process of the line edit occurs as often as necessary with a publishing house. However, with a freelancer you need to ask up front how many times it will go back and forth.

Copy editing involves going line-by-line through a manuscript to correct grammar, punctuation, word usage, and consistency issues. A copy edit should be done after line editing.

The Full Edit or Complete Edit combines both the developmental and line edits. The developmental is completed first. Once you have fixed the big-picture items, the manuscript goes back for the line edit. The process of the full edit can and does take place at a publishing house.

It's important to do these edits in the correct order. Doing a line edit before a big-picture is like putting shingles on a roof without the underlying framework. Big-picture issues should always be fixed first. If you've asked for a line edit, there are some people who may not tell you your book has structural issues. However, reputable editors will tell you if there are major problems that need fixed before completing a line edit.

## Choosing an Editor

When hiring a freelancer, ask your writer friends if they can recommend anyone. Find out about the editor's experience, specialty, and training. Then interview your choices by phone or video, if possible. As far as cost is concerned, it varies widely. The Writer's Digest *Writer's Market Guide* includes a pricing chart that gives high, low, and average costs for all things writing related. The book can generally be found in the reference section of your library. You might want to review "Why Should I Hire an Editor?"

Many editors offer a sample edit of the first chapter. Some charge for this and others offer it free. This gives the writer an idea of how the editor works, and it helps the editor see some of the writer's strengths and weaknesses.

As you can see, this process can get lengthy. Time to complete an edit depends on how much and what type of work is to be done. It's also subject to the freelancer's workload.

Of course, you can't pick the person a publishing house assigns to your book, but you can do your best to make that relationship work.

At some point, you may find yourself getting frustrated. So what can you do?

First of all, take several days break from the project. Don't even think about it, and especially do not rehearse the problems in your head. That will only make your frustration grow. Turn your attention to something else and allow your emotions and frustration to subside. When you're ready to go back to the project, pray for insight, wisdom, and clear communication. Do your best to determine what's frustrating you. Are the editor's instructions unclear? Is your voice disappearing? Are changes being made that you didn't ask to be done?

Once you've outlined the problem(s), then draft an email or request a phone conversation to discuss things. Worst case scenario, you terminate your work with that freelancer, but we'll take a closer look at choices a bit later.

For now, let's dive into how you can help your editor as well as minimize the frustration level.

## Author Attitude

We all know our attitude toward anything in life is important. Winston Churchill was especially inspiring when he said, "Attitude is a little thing that makes a big difference."

To be successful you must be willing to do everything you can to make your book the best it can be and to make it a success. That includes understanding that the editor is not your enemy. Rejection in publishing is inevitable. In fact, if a writer told me she had never received a rejection letter, I'd say she had never submitted any work or very little.

Whether you're working with a publishing house editor or a freelancer, that person is going to give feedback and suggest or make changes. A writer who makes an excuse about every change is a warning flag for the editor. It means the writer doesn't have what I call a teachable spirit.

> "Attitude is a little thing that makes a big difference."
> ~ Winston Churchill

In writing, we must be willing to learn and grow, and I believe your skill with words will grow in direct relation to how well you accept and apply feedback about your work. If you've hired a freelancer, but ignore what he says, you're wasting your money — and I've yet to meet a writer who has bags of that lying around.

Take the pain out of your edit by adopting the approach that your editor is an advocate for your story. Listen to what he has to say and put those tips into practice. It will make your writing that much stronger.

# How Can You Help Your Editor?

As you enter the editing process, learn how the editor prefers to communicate. Does she prefer email only or are phone calls okay? Is she open to video calls? Ask what you can do to help.

And pray for her. Editing is as solitary work as writing. Pray for wisdom and insight as she works, for her health, her family. Be bold and ask if she has any specifics you can pray about. When I get an email from a client saying she's praying for me, it encourages me, especially after a tough day.

One of the best things you can do for your editor besides praying is to make your manuscript as clean as possible. Run a spell check. Carefully read through your story one more time looking for missing/misplaced commas and quote marks. Make sure you have opening and closing quotations on your dialogue. Look for those squiggly red and green lines MS Word puts into your writing. Those indicate spelling and grammar issues. Read your manuscript like you were proofing the galleys in preparation for printing, and fix every error you see. Then prepare a style sheet.

"What's a style sheet?" you ask.

This document provides the details of your story, such as setting (Coffeeville or Coffeyville), character names (especially if spelled in an unusual way) and physical descriptions. Slang, idioms, jargon and foreign words you use. Grammar and writing rules you break and why. Also helpful is source documentation for quotations so the editor can check for accuracy.

One last item that can help both you and the editor is to learn how to use track changes. This is most likely the tool editors will use in a line edit. Here's a link to a video provided by LinkedIn on YouTube: https://www.youtube.com/watch?v=5_knruAysnA&t.

## Your Choices in the Editing Process

Your manuscript is back from the editor along with the report. Now what? Every publishing house has their own process. Bigger houses may have one person who handles the developmental edit and another who does line and copy editing. Small houses may have one person who does it all. No matter who handles your edit, you have three choices.

1. **Make the suggested changes.** You agree with a suggested change and see how it improves the story. You'll make the change without doubt.

2. **Compromise.** You realize there's a problem with an element of your book, but are not sure the editor's solution is the right one. Work to find a compromise. It goes both ways. Editors need to listen to an author's reasonable objections and explanations. In a manuscript CrossRiver Media accepted, the religious sect of the main characters was an unfamiliar one to us. When we voiced concern about some of what was said and done in the story, the author explained the doctrine and we accepted it.

3. **Refuse the change(s).** Just as you can accept some or all changes, you can also refuse them. Realize, however, refusal of some changes can jeopardize publication. Many publishing contracts contain clauses about delivering a manuscript in an acceptable form and refusal to make changes the publisher feels are essential may open the door for the publisher to cancel the contract.

These same choices are available to you when you work with a

freelancer. If the editorial report upsets you, set the project aside for several days to allow your emotions to cool down. During that time ask God for insight into what's causing your frustration.

When you're ready, draft an email outlining your concerns, or request a phone call. If you talk by phone, prepare a list of bullet points ahead of time to help remind you of everything. Don't be afraid to ask questions, but be prepared to explain why you disagree with changes. You've done the hard work in writing the book, but now as an editor joins the publication journey, the process becomes a joint effort.

In a post on Writer Unboxed, author Juliet Marillier says, "Don't lose sight of the fact that this is your book. Your plot. Your characters. Your story. Do listen to your editor's wise advice, but if you know in your heart of hearts that a particular revision is just wrong, and that no compromise is possible, explain this to your editor. Don't justify it with a gush of emotion, back it up with sound arguments."

One last thing…Meet your deadlines. If something occurs and you know you can't meet it, notify your editor as soon as possible to work out something else. Your book isn't the only book the publishing house or freelancer has in process. Allowing your deadline to blow on by can cause a ripple effect in the workload and is disrespectful of the time and effort of others involved.

Now that you know what's involved in the professional editing process and what it costs, here are seven cheat sheets that will help you write a better book and reduce the final cost of a freelance edit. Though you are certainly free to hop to whichever cheat sheet you need most, I've put them in a special order, the order in which you should review your manuscript. Checking for the little things is a waste of time if afterward you make major revision to the text.

# Cheat Sheet #1
# Helpful Websites for Research

*The full URLs of all links referenced in this cheat sheet can be found in Reference Links at the end of this book.*

**H**ave you ever stopped reading a book because you spotted a factual error? At a recent writers' conference, the keynote speaker (a writer and editor) started off with a story about what makes him stop reading a book. His hobby is grafting trees. The main character in a book he was reading grafted trees, but the author of the book made a mistake in the proper procedure for grafting.

That error caused the keynote speaker to doubt the author's credibility. He closed the book and never finished it.

Imagine reading a nonfiction book and the author makes an error concerning the topic of the book! Readers put a book down for a multitude of reasons. Don't let sloppy research — or none at all — be the reason readers stop reading your book.

The most costly and #1 way research affects the author is when acquisition editors peruse your book proposal. If those editors spot factual errors in your proposal or manuscript, they'll hesitate to look further. They'll wonder, How many other errors has this author made? A literary agent will react the same way. Don't risk having your proposal rejected because of poor research.

Yes, time doing research can be extensive, especially if you write historical fiction. If you write about the same era, eventually, you won't spend as much time because your knowledge accumulates. Keep good records of your sources so you can go back to them when you write the next book.

You won't use every bit of research you unearth, but all that information helps you create a seamless story with depth that keeps the reader engaged and turning the pages. A word of warning here: Don't attempt to work in all your research. It will come across forced and obvious to the reader.

You might be tempted think you don't need to do any research for your book. If so, visit my blog The Motivational Editor and read "Why Research Matters." Here is another post from my blog that will help: "Don't Make These Mistakes in Doing Research."

There are a wide variety of source documents available when it comes to research. Understanding what they're called can help as you seek out your information.

*Primary source documents* are firsthand accounts, such as actual letters, diaries/journals, speeches, photographs, and documents. They are the best sources, especially for historical fiction. There also *secondary* and *tertiary sources*. Read "Primary and Secondary Sources" from the Ithaca College Library for more detail on what each is. Here are starting points for your research...

- The Reference Desk of the Internet, *the* place for facts and stats, and, oh, so much more

- Official state websites are especially helpful with historical sites within a state. You may find photographs, climate and typography info, maps, etc.
- The National Archives, a government site, is an excellent place to start for primary source docs relating to American history.
- The Library of Congress
- Librarians Index to the Internet (This site is no longer being updated, but is still usable.)
- HighBeam Encyclopedia
- WWW Virtual Library
- Princeton University Library

Many sites are topic specific.

- EyeWitness to History
- CyberPursuits, Anthropology
- History.com
- Life magazine photo archive, hosted by Google
- DocsTeach (Designed for teachers and run by the National Archives, but this site provides links to primary source documents.)
- The Avalon Project, a source for global history from Yale University
- For governmental topics, try USA.gov
- Does one of your characters have a specific illness or physical condition? Try WebMD.com or MayoClinic.org.

If you write thrillers, the CIA World Factbook might be useful. This site is chock full of factual information about the countries of the world.

## Search engines

There are search engines... and there are meta-search engines. Search engines create an index/database of the sites they crawl. When you do a search, the engine searches its database and returns the results to you. Google is a search engine. And there's no denying Google has captured the search engine market, but there are sites beyond Google that offer more choices.

- Ask.com
- Gigablast

## Meta-search Engines

A meta-search engine doesn't create its own index. Instead it utilizes the indexes of other search engines. So when you use a meta-search engine, you're getting results from several search engines. To help you understand the difference between a search engine and a meta-search engine, here's an analogy. A search engine is like getting results from every book in the public library system in your state. A meta-search engine would get results from every library in the world. A meta-search engine also offers a more finely tuned results page.

- Ixquick, (unlike Google, they don't collect personal information as you search)
- Dogpile
- DuckDuckGo
- Yippy

## How Does Research Affect the Editor?

# 7 CHEAT SHEETS TO CUT EDITING COSTS

In my position as editor at CrossRiver, it's up to me to verify the accuracy of facts, quotes, and historical data. The writer's research saves me hours of searching in my efforts to verify that information — provided the same writer sends me his or her list of source material. That material provides what I need to proof quotes, facts, accuracy of the story time line, and more.

You may think I'm exaggerating when I say research saves me hours of work, but I'm not. Historical fiction writers often weave in true events, and I have to verify that what they say is accurate — right down to whether the $100 bill existed in 1859. Sometimes it's a typo, but often it is a misstatement of fact. Nonfiction books cover topics I know nothing about. That makes the author's source material critical as I edit.

Larger publishing houses may have fact checkers or assign this task to proofreaders, but no matter who does it, verification has to be done or you risk publishing an error.

Provide your editor with a document of all your source material, complete with links and book titles.

*Great research makes a difference.*

# Cheat Sheet #2
# Point of View (POV)

**D**efined, point of view is perspective. Through whose eyes are we seeing the story, whose head are we inside of, and whose emotions do we experience as the character experiences them?

But with POV comes an age-old struggle. Should I write my novel in first or third person (or get wild and crazy and use second person)? Am I limited to a single character, or can I use multiple points of view? Who should my novel's POV character be?

Have you asked yourself any of those questions? Many writers do, especially beginning writers.

You want to write a story readers can't put down, but how do you decide which POV is the best so you can increase your chances of writing a best-selling novel? In fact, how can you even begin to write without having decided this basic element?

Let's take a look at the options.

# First person
## telling your story from the point of "I."

*As I stared at the ominous black clouds forming in the west, my heart began to pound. I'd learned to fear tornadoes the hard way.*

You can achieve more emotional intimacy with this POV, but the entire story is then normally told from the perspective of that one character. (This isn't a rule.) We aren't privy to the thoughts of any other character, and we experience the emotions of other characters by what the POV character sees and hears.

# Third person subjective
## he/she/it, fully experiencing the thoughts and emotions of the POV character.

*As she stared at the ominous black clouds forming in the west, her heart began to pound. She'd learned to fear tornadoes the hard way.*

This is the most popular POV and has greater versatility than first person, though it doesn't make quite the same emotional connection. Compare this example with the first-person example above for a feel of the difference in emotional connection.

# Third person objective
## he/she/it, detached from the character's emotions and thoughts.

*She looked at the black clouds forming in the west. She had experienced tornadoes as a child.*

To me, third person objective is devoid of emotion and

boring, but this may serve your purposes.

## Second person
### telling your story from the point of "you."

*As you stare at the ominous black clouds forming in the west, your heart begins to pound. You learned to fear tornadoes the hard way.*

Many readers struggle to read this point of view, myself included. It makes me feel as though someone is controlling me. If you are a beginning writer, I suggest you avoid this POV for now. Master first or third person before you attempt second.

## Omniscient
### all-knowing narrator whose voice is as distinctive as any character in the story.

*As she stared at the black ominous clouds forming in the west, her heart began to pound. Like most of us living in Tornado Alley, she had learned to fear tornadoes the hard way.*

When not done properly omniscient POV comes out as head-hopping, jumping from one character's thoughts and emotions to another's within the same scene. (Head-hopping is acceptable in the romance genre because the relationship is considered the main character.) Study *The Princess Bride*, *Gone with the Wind*, or *A Tale of Two Cities* for omni-POV done well.

Though once popular, many publishers don't want omni-POV. But like all things retro, it is gaining popularity once again.

# Who Is the Best Character to Tell Your Story?

No story has just one character. Even in a plot of one man against nature, nature becomes the second character. So how can you determine who is your best POV character?

Think about what happens to each character and how much you want to reveal about them along the way.

Most often the main POV character is the protagonist. But are there aspects of your protagonist that can only be revealed via an objective character's POV? *The Great Gatsby* utilizes a POV that is not the protagonist. This character reveals aspects of Gatsby's character that Gatsby would have never seen about himself.

Does your protagonist have secrets you don't want your reader to know until the end of the story?

Then avoid first person. Readers expect full access to the thoughts and emotions of a first-person POV character. Because there is a degree of emotional detachment in third person you can keep some thoughts and emotions secret in order to serve your plot. For that reason, third person is best for mysteries and thrillers. Part of the wonderful versatility of third person is its ability for you to zoom in on a character's thoughts and emotions or zoom out to whatever emotional distance you desire.

Harper Lee's *To Kill a Mockingbird* is a wonderful example of how a story can differ with character perspective. Consider the occupations of your characters and how that could impact the story you tell. Is there a character, whether child or adult, who would provide a more interesting take on your story?

Is it important that readers experience the thoughts and emotions of more than one of your characters?

Then third person is probably your best option. Some genres (and some publishers) require a specific point of view.

Review other books in your genre for their POV.

Each option has its benefits and drawbacks. Consider your plot, the protagonist's character arc, and what you plan to reveal at the end. Ask yourself lots of questions about your story and characters as you ponder POV. I especially like Nancy Kress's advice in her book *Characters, Emotion & Viewpoint*: "Whose head are you most interested in inhabiting during this story?"

## In a Quandary? Then Experiment.

Take one scene from your story and write it in first person with the protagonist. Then write that same scene in third person.

Now try writing that same scene with a different character other than your protagonist. Which was easier to write? Which one seems to flow more smoothly. Read each one out loud. Which sounds best?

As you learn the craft of writing and develop your skills, it's best to master point of view with one character throughout your story (whether through first or third person) before moving on to multiple POV characters or experimenting with the more demanding second person and omniscient POVs.

There are other ways of handling POV than those I've covered here. I recommend reading *Unmasking the Mystery of Point of View* by Angela Hunt, and *Characters, Emotions & Viewpoint* by Nancy Kress for a more in depth discussion of point of view.

By giving POV greater thought before you begin writing, you can have a stronger story from page 1.

# Cheat Sheet #3
# Show versus Tell

**W**riters often hear "show us, don't tell us" in one variation or another. But what does that mean?

*Merriam-Webster's Unabridged Dictionary* gives the definition of *tell* as "to relate in detail: narrate, recount," and *show* as "to cause or permit to be seen." As writers, we do both these things. But as storytellers we must recount our tale in a way that allows the reader to experience what our story characters see and feel. We must paint a picture with our words.

Let's look at some examples.

*Sally could see Cade was very angry with her answer.*

This tells us only that Sally sees Cade and that he is very angry. It doesn't show us exactly what Sally sees that allows her to conclude Cade is angry or exactly what Cade experiences physically.

*Sally watched Cade as the vein on the left side of his neck began to bulge and pulse with each beat of his heart. Inch by inch his face turned deep red as rage welled within him.*

Now you have shown us exactly what Sally sees and what Cade is experiencing/feeling. Showing often takes more words to express, but would you rather experience the story or fall asleep?

Read each example sentence again. How differently do you see and feel as you read each one?

Showing provides strong verbs and descriptors that help the reader visualize what's happening. Showing pulls us into the story and we experience — have our own emotional and physical response — what the characters are experiencing.

Telling uses weak verbs (and usually linking verbs with them) and lacks the verbal clues a reader needs to imagine the scene. Telling is flat, black and white writing.

## Show or tell, but not both

This mistake might be the most difficult for new writers to spot because they haven't fully grasped the difference between telling and showing. Sometimes telling is what you need, but you don't use both to express the same thought at the same moment. Providing both insults the reader's intelligence.

*It was obvious he was embarrassed. I worked to stifle my smile as a crimson blush crept up his neck.*

The first sentence tells. The second sentence shows. We don't need both. Here's another example accomplished in one sentence.

*I was so angry I slammed my fist down on the table.*

Again, the first portion tells, the second half shows. Even if you shifted the sentence order, you're still making the same mistake.

You, as the writer, are the best judge of whether showing or telling is what you need depending on the effect you're trying to establish. I'm not an advocate of all show, no tell. Scribophile provides an excellent post, "The Show Versus Tell Debate," that explains the maxim.

## How to Fix Telling vs. Showing

Discovering where your story tells rather than shows isn't always that easy because we constantly have the scene playing out in our mind as we write.

Look for sentences that use verbs with linking verbs (e.g. could see, was angry). The word *was* is often an indicator of telling. Here is an example from a friend's manuscript.

*He was comfortable with his air of superiority; he wore it well, punctuated by a subtle sneer.*

This sentence has some great elements, but part of it was telling. Here's how I reworked it.

*He wore his air of superiority comfortably and punctuated it with a subtle sneer.*

Participate in a critique group. They won't see the same thing you do as they read your scenes. If you don't have a critique group, put your finished manuscript aside for at least a month or two. When you come back to it, can you richly visualize what's happening or do the scenes seems flat?

Ask some friends who are avid readers to read your story

and give honest feedback.

Be an avid reader yourself. Analyze what you read for telling vs. showing.

# Cheat Sheet #4
# Checklist of
# Chicago Manual of Style

he advent of word processing changed how we format certain items in our writing. But let me first cover the standard format for your manuscript and then I'll cover some specific items like book titles.

Writers submit their manuscripts to me in all sorts of fancy fonts. But guess what. Those fancy fonts are hard to read. Editors want to read a fantastic story, not go blind.

Before you submit your story to a literary agent or publisher, format it in the following way:

- Times New Roman regular (not bold or italic), 12 pt
- Double spaced
- First line indent (See "How to Create the Smartest Indent for Manuscripts" on my blog)

- Use the page break to separate your chapters, not lots of paragraph returns (See "A Better, Easier Way to Create a Page Break" on my blog).
- There is only one space between sentences. Do a find and replace to fix it.

## Formatting Guidelines for Your Story

In the world of publishing, there are two books on writing style that pull a lot of muscle. In the book world, *The Chicago Manual of Style* is the primary style guide. This book contains over 1000 pages and instructs on how to handle everything from what to italicize to how to properly use punctuation.

For newspapers and periodicals, *The Associated Press Style Guide* holds sway. Let's not forget *The Christian Writer's Manual of Style*, used by many Christian publishing houses.

I own all three. These aren't books you need to purchase, but learning some of the basics will go a long way in cutting your editing costs. Look for these books in your library if you want to see what they're like. I'm presenting the most common items here to help you learn them.

## What Titles to Italicize

- Books
- Magazines
- Names of websites
- CD albums
- Movies
- TV shows

- Radio programs and radio series
- Plays
- Operas and long musical compositions
- Paintings, drawings, photographs, and other works of art
- Names of newspapers, both domestic and foreign
- Long poems (Dante's *Inferno*)
- Cartoons and comic strips that occur regularly, such as *Peanuts*
- Words you want to emphasize

This isn't a complete list, but it will answer the majority of your questions about titles.

## Using Quotation Marks Aside from Dialogue

- For a single song title and TV and radio episodes
- Most poems (unless it falls into the long category)
- Chapter titles
- Article titles (includes blog post titles)
- Text directly quoted from other works. Be sure to cite your source either within the text or with a footnote or endnote. See "More Information on Fair Use" at Copyright.gov to learn about the Fair Use Act and about quoting other documents.

## Should I Use a Numeral or Spell It Out?

- If writing a book, spell out numbers zero through one hundred. (*Chicago Manual* standard)

- If writing for newspapers or periodicals, spell out single digit numbers. (*Associated Press* standard)
- The above two guidelines also apply to currency.
- If a number begins the sentence, always spell it out.
- When expressing percentages, numerals are used. In general text use percent — Fewer than 10 percent of writers know these rules. In scientific and statistical works use the symbol %.

## Times of day

- For whole, quarter, and half hours spell out — I boarded the plane at one thirty.
- When using o'clock, always spell out — My appointment is at nine o'clock.
- When precise time is required use numerals — The train leaves at 5:52 a.m.

## Capitalization

This is another area writers struggle with, often capitalizing needlessly. I realize it's difficult to remember all the rules, but here's a guideline: Is the word a proper name or is it a generic term?

Here are some examples:

- Is Sir Michael heading the expedition? (the official British title used with name)
- "Yes, sir, I'm headed there now." (generic)
- I'm scheduled for Algebra 101 for this semester. (official course name)

- I'm scheduled for algebra this semester. (generic)

## Caveat

In most cases these guidelines will serve you well and give your manuscript a professional look. Like everything, there are exceptions to the rules — let the publisher worry about those.

Also be aware that publishers and periodicals choose the style guide they prefer. In addition, they often have what's called house style. House styles are exceptions to the general style guide. They are rules you won't know unless they tell you: "We follow the *Christian Writer's Manual of Style* in that we capitalize pronouns referring to God."

Don't let these guides get in your way as you write your draft. Once you enter the final revision stages and prep your book for a professional editor or for submission, then review your manuscript for these items and correct them.

# Cheat Sheet #5
# Punctuation Guidelines

"**I** don't understand all those rules and I don't want to."

"Let editors worry about the correct punctuation."

"I just want to write, not worry about where to put a comma."

Do you see yourself in the above sentences? If you don't, you are probably in the minority.

The comma, period, colon, em dash, and all those other punctuation marks have their function. I think the only one that doesn't confuse writers is the period. Here are guidelines on the most common elements of punctuation.

## Comma or No Comma?

There are those of you who prefer to let editors or proof-readers worry about commas, but if you're hiring a freelancer,

learning some punctuation basics will save you money because the editor will spend less time fixing incorrect commas in your manuscript.

I'll be the first to say the rules governing the English language are confusing. I've often wondered why there seems to be an exception to every rule — sometimes two or three. I reference my *Chicago Manual of Style* regularly. I also spend time in my *Grammar Desk Reference* learning the whys and wherefores of grammar so I can correctly punctuate a sentence.

Here are some guidelines for commas I see most misused. Don't worry, I'll make it easy by avoiding all the impossible-to-remember grammatical terms.

Should I write…

*Her ex-husband Bert lives in Florida.*

*Her ex-husband, Bert, lives in Florida.*

The sentence without the commas tells us this woman has more than one ex-husband. Bert is essential to the sentence so we know which one is being discussed.

If the woman in your story only has one ex-hubby, then include the commas. The name Bert isn't essential for us to know who the ex is, but offers us additional info about the one and only ex-husband. Here are two more examples:

*My twin sister, Dot, lives in Kansas.*

The name Dot is not essential to the sentence — I can have only one twin.

*My brother Mark lives in the land of fruits and nuts.*

Mark is essential to the sentence because I have more than one brother. Ask yourself whether that extra bit of info is essential for the reader to know exactly who you're talking about. If it is, then no commas are needed.

## Then

The word *then*, when used at the beginning of a sentence, is rarely set off with a comma (did I mention there are always exceptions?).

*Incorrect: Then, I sat down with a thud.*

*Correct: Then I sat down with a thud.*

## And, but, yet, or, nor, for

These words are most often used as conjunctions — sorry, can't avoid the grammatical term on this one.

*Sally cried all night, and Max laughed for having scared her.*

When you use *and, but, yet, or, nor,* or *for* at the beginning of a sentence, do not use a comma.

*Sally cried all night. And Max laughed for having scared her.*

By the way, it's perfectly all right to begin a sentence with these words. When I'm in a hurry and don't want to dig through my grammar reference or style manual, I visit Grammar Girl, Mignon Fogarty, over at QuickandDirtyTips.com

# The Oxford Comma, aka Serial Comma

The Oxford comma is the comma that comes before a conjunction when you have three or more items in a series. And in the world of publishing, the *Chicago Manual of Style* rules. A quote from the manual: Chicago strongly recommends this widely practiced usage.

*For breakfast I ate a baked potato topped with chili, broccoli, and cheese.*

If you write for magazines and newspapers, they traditionally follow the *Associated Press* style, which doesn't use the serial comma. But the serial comma can help your reader avoid misunderstanding.

*Incorrect: My three favorite desserts are chocolate chip cookies, ice cream with chocolate syrup and peanuts and cherry pie.*

Written this way it says I put cherry pie on my ice cream along with syrup and peanuts.

*Correct: My three favorite desserts are chocolate chip cookies, ice cream with chocolate syrup and peanuts, and cherry pie.*

# The Em Dash

This dash is so named because it is the same width as the letter *m*. You create it by typing two dashes together without

any space between them. Most word processing programs will then auto-format it once you hit the next key, be it the space bar or first letter of the next word.

In MS Word and Scrivener (for Windows), the keyboard shortcut is Alt+0151 (I love keyboard shortcuts, don't you?).

The em dash indicates a dramatic shift in tone or thought within a sentence. Do not use an em dash as you would a comma.

> *His marriage proposal — would she say no? — got caught in his throat as he began.*

When used in pairs, the portion set off by the em dash gets the most emphasis. In other words, that portion stands out as the most important part of the sentence.

The em dash can also be used as a single dash.

> *His marriage proposal got caught in his throat before he began — would she say no?*

When you want to indicate an interruption in dialogue, use an em dash.

> *"Of course, she'll —"*
> *"Say yes," John finished Mickey's sentence.*

Writer's Digest *Grammar Desk Reference* states the em dash "is the most dramatic punctuation mark you can deploy within the interior of a sentence. Use it sparingly."

Like the exclamation mark, overuse negates *its* power.

## The Ellipsis

Before computers, the ellipsis (three periods together) had a space between each period. This is another item word processors auto-format. Type three periods in a row without the space between them.

In dialogue the ellipsis indicates that the speaker hasn't finished his or her words or shows a pause.

> "I'm not...I don't..." Mark stammered to his friend. "What if she says...no to my marriage proposal?"

To show that one or more words have been omitted from a direct quote, use an ellipsis.

> The mayor said that "the working citizens...lose 37 percent of their paycheck to taxes."

The ellipsis indicates the mayor spoke something more in between "citizens" and "lose" that was irrelevant to the quoter's purpose. Never omit words that will change the meaning of the original quote.

## The Colon

While the colon is not as common as the punctuation above, I see it often enough to include here.

My *Grammar Desk Reference* states, "The colon is an introducer." It points the reader to more information.

> *Incorrect: My three favorite desserts: chocolate chip*

*cookies, ice cream with chocolate syrup, and cherry pie.*

*Correct: Most often I choose three items over any other for dessert: chocolate chip cookies, ice cream with chocolate syrup, and cherry pie.*

The text preceding a colon must be a complete sentence.

# Cheat Sheet #6
# Ten Basic Steps for
# Self-Editing Fiction

**W**hether you outline or write by the seat of your pants, you need to start your self-editing with big picture items. Whole books have been written that cover self-editing. This cheat sheet gives you the basics to get you started. Except for #1 and #10, the order in which you examine these items is strictly up to you.

## 1. Let Your Manuscript Rest

After completing your draft, step away from your story for a month (or at least a week). Give yourself enough time to forget all those little details your brain thinks it included. Then read the whole thing through from the perspective of a reader reading it for the first time. Take notes on things you notice.

### 2. Examine Plot

- What is your protagonist's story goal?
- What conflicts does he/she meet throughout the story?
- Do those conflicts grow in intensity?
- What is the climax of the plot?
- How does your protagonist deal with the climatic event?
- What is the denouement, aka resolution?

### 3. Examine Story Characters

- Are they well rounded, three dimensional? Do you show physical, emotional, mental, and back story aspects of your characters?
- Does the protagonist have flaws?
- Does the antagonist have at least one likable attribute?
- Can your reader bond with the protagonist?
- Are your characters acting and reacting in ways that seem forced or natural for that character?

### 4. Point of View

- Are you consistent with POV in every scene?
- If writing in first person, can that character actually see and feel what you are describing?
- Are you head hopping—describing the thoughts of other characters.

### 5. Story Setting and Mood

- Have you set the story stage? Where does your story take place? If you write fantasy, examine this closely.

- If writing historical fiction, setting the story time is essential.
- Do you use words that help set the mood of the story/scene?

## 6. Show Versus Tell

- There is a time for both.
- Show must far outweigh tell.

## 7. Dialogue

- Is the dialogue natural?
- Can you differentiate the characters by their dialogue?
- Do you have too much or not enough?
- How does the dialogue of your scenes contribute to story advancement?

Visit my blog to read about nine aspects of dialogue from best-selling author Cecil Murphey.

## 8. Scenes

Like your book, and like chapters, every scene needs a beginning, middle, and end. Can you pick them out?

- Are the right characters showing up in your scenes?
- Is there some kind of conflict to every scene?
- How does each scene advance the story?
- Does the pace of each scene fit what's happening in the scene? An action-packed scene is going to be fast paced (more short sentences).

### 9. Theme

Not all authors include theme in their stories.
- If you have a theme, what is it?
- Were you able to identify that theme in your first read through?
- Did another theme seem to present itself as you wrote the story? If so, what did you do with it?
- Have you used thematic elements or are you preaching your theme?

### 10. Finally, after you've made revisions that fix the big picture issues, it's time to line edit.

- Read line by line ensuring you've used the right word to communicate what's needed
- That modifiers are in the right place
- That pronouns have the correct antecedents
- That you've used correct grammar, spelling, and punctuation

I often like to print out a manuscript I'm editing. It's amazing what you see on the printed page that you don't notice on the screen. And you can make all kinds of notes on a printed copy that you can't as easily mark online.

# Cheat Sheet #7
# Seven Basic Steps to
# Self-Editing Nonfiction

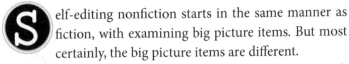

**S**elf-editing nonfiction starts in the same manner as fiction, with examining big picture items. But most certainly, the big picture items are different.

Aside from #1 and #7, the order in which you examine each of these elements is entirely up to you.

**1. Let it rest a month or so.**

After completing your draft, step away from your book for a month (or at least a week). Give yourself enough time to forget all those little details your brain thinks it included. Then read the whole thing through from the perspective of a reader reading it for the first time. Read it out loud. You'll notice more that way. Take notes on what needs fixed.

## 2. Structure

How is your book laid out?

- Is the structure of your book appropriate for its purpose (i.e. entertain, inform, stimulate, persuade)?
- In chapters only, or is your topic conducive to parts as well?
- Are there sections to each chapter? If so, are any missing?

## 3. Organization

- Is there logic to your organization?
- Do chapter openings hook the reader?
- Do chapters end well and transition well to the next?

What is the reader going to learn/glean from reading your book? This is what's called the "takeaway" value of your book.

- Are the audience and takeaway apparent?

For Example: In my book *Carried by Grace: a Guide for Mothers of Sexual Abuse Victims*, it would not have made sense or been helpful to the reader to start the book with a chapter about divorce. The topic lent itself to a "from the very beginning, day-by-day" approach. Thus, for organization, I started with the shock a mother experiences when she learns her child has been abused, and then organized each following chapter in an order that the events played out.

When it came to structure, each chapter started with a bit of my story to introduce the topic of the chapter and connect with the reader in a way that said "I know you're hurting. I've been there too." Then came a devotional reading, action steps, and a prayer.

Your book may not lend itself to this type of structure and

organization, but as you self-edit, ask yourself if you've chosen what's best for the topic and reader engagement.

## 4. Flow

- Does each chapter topic flow naturally from one to the other?
- Does each paragraph flow smoothly one to the other with appropriate transitions?

Realize in self-editing nonfiction that structure, organization, and flow are almost as tightly knit as bone is to marrow. Jotting down the main idea of each part and chapter will help you determine if your organization and flow is correct. (Oops, that sounds like making an outline.)

## 5. Research/Charts/Images

- Have you correctly cited all your sources?
- Have you logged all your sources? I learned the hard way to copy/paste URLs immediately. I've wanted to reread a web page later on and couldn't find it anymore.
- Have you requested and acquired all necessary copyright permissions?
- Are your charts/images relevant, accurate, and readable?
- Are anecdotes and examples understandable, interesting, and relevant?

## 6. Finally, after you've made revisions that fix the big picture issues, it's time to line edit.

Read line by line ensuring you've...

- Used just the right word to communicate what's needed
- That modifiers are in the right place
- That pronouns have the correct antecedents
- That you've used correct grammar, spelling, and punctuation.

**7. Read through it from start to finish again as if reading it for the first time.**

It's easy to edit a sentence and in the process mess up previous or following sentences. A standard read-through will help you catch stuff like that.

Once you've completed these steps, you're ready for a professional edit.

# Cheat Sheet Bonus
# Ten Things to Do Before
# You Hire an Editor

**1** Look for passive voice, and revise to active where appropriate. (There is a right time to use passive. See my blog post "Is it ever okay to use passive voice?") You can set MS Word to show grammar errors. I found that particularly helpful in learning to recognize passive voice. If you remember your elementary school English, the subject of the sentence takes action on the object of the sentence. Subject — verb — object. In passive voice that order is reversed: object — verb — subject.

Passive voice example: The bank was robbed by John Doe.
Better written: John Doe robbed the bank.
If you don't know who robbed the bank, you most likely will use passive voice. The bank was robbed.

**2** Review for telling, She felt embarressed. — and revise to showing — Heat flooded her face as she realized her faux pas.

**3** Watch out for repetition in description. Tell us two, maybe three times that your character has auburn hair, but not every time you mention her hair.

**4** Avoid repetition of words — smiled, laughed, chuckled, cried, etc. Watch out for crutch words, too. We all have them: well, so, but, always, also, too, and others. To find them, do a word search and use reading highlights in Word. If you use Scrivener, take advantage of text statistics.

**5** Look for adverb/verb combinations. A word search for *ly* will help. In these cases, with patience and perseverance, you can discover one verb to replace both words and make your sentence stronger, your writing tighter. When my brain struggles to find the best word, I turn to OneLook Reverse Dictionary.

**6** Make sure you aren't head hopping.

**7** Is there adequate conflict and tension? Without it, your story is boring.

**8** Watch for weak verbs such as "talking," and "walking." Replace with active verbs. In these examples, "she jabbered, he sauntered." Do a word search on *was, were, has, am, are, is* to help find weak verbs.

**9** Format your manuscript correctly. Times New Roman, 12 pt, double spaced, with first line indent. And in this digital age, there is only one space after sentences. See my blog post "How to create the smartest indent for manuscripts."

**10** Make your manuscript as clean as you can. Check for spelling, punctuation, grammar, and typos. Do a search on homonyms (words that sound alike, but are spelled differently and have different meanings) such as two, too, and to; they're, their, and there. Read the context and ensure you've used the correct word. One word I see consistently spelled wrong is the past tense of the verb *lead*, as in to lead a sheep to slaughter, because led sounds like the mineral lead.

# Wrapping it up

**Y**ou might be tempted to sit back and relax once you've sent your manuscript for a professional edit. Allow yourself a few days' breather, but then while you wait for your editor to complete the work, focus in on the next steps. If your book is under publishing contract, fine tune your marketing strategy and devise your marketing plans. If you've hired a freelance editor, now is the time to complete your book proposal, if you haven't already, and search for potential publishers or agents.

When you begin work on your next book, re-examine the editorial feedback from your previous book. Make a list of consistent problems such as POV or plot development and use it to refine your writing. Once your newest draft is complete, review it for those same issues and revise as needed.

Attend workshops at writers conferences or consider taking an online course for topics you struggle with. Reread

books you especially like and study how those writers handle the areas you need to develop. Learn from the editor's advice and apply it to all future work.

In conclusion, remember you are an active participant in the editing process. The goal is to have the best book possible. One that will appeal to readers and be worth buying — and that means royalties in your pocket.

# Reference Links

DebraLButterfield.com

## Debra's Articles

**"Why Research Matters:"** http://debralbutterfield.com/research-matters-novel/
**"Don't Make These Mistakes in Doing Research:"** http://debralbutterfield.com/mistakes-in-doing-research/
**"How to Create the Smartest Indent for Manuscripts:"** (the first line indent): http://debralbutterfield.com/create-indents/)
**"A Better, Easier Way to Create a Page Break:"**
http://debralbutterfield.com/create-page-break/

## Research Websites

**Ithaca College Library, Primary and Secondary Sources:**

https://library.ithaca.edu/sp/subjects/primary

**The Reference Desk of the Internet:** http://www.refdesk.com/

**The National Archives:** https://www.archives.gov/

**The Library of Congress:** https://www.loc.gov/

**Librarians Index to the Internet:** http://www.ipl.org/ (This site is no longer being updated, but is still usable.)

**HighBeam Encyclopedia:** http://www.encyclopedia.com/

**WWW Virtual Library:** http://vlib.org/

**Princeton University Library Finding Aids:**
http://findingaids.princeton.edu/

**EyeWitness to History:** http://www.eyewitnesstohistory.com/

**CyberPursuits, Anthropology:** http://www.cyberpursuits.com/anthro/

**History.com:** http://www.history.com/

*Life* **magazine photo archive hosted by Google:** http://images.google.com/hosted/life

**DocsTeach** (designed for teachers and run by the National Archives, but this site provides links to primary source documents): https://www.docsteach.org/documents

**The Avalon Project,** a source for global history from Yale University: http://avalon.law.yale.edu/

**Web MD:** http://www.webmd.com/

**Mayo Clinic:** http://www.mayoclinic.org/

**USA.gov:** https://www.usa.gov/

**CIA World Factbook:** https://www.cia.gov/library/publications/the-world-factbook/index.html

## Search and Meta Search Engines

**Google**.com
**Ask**.com
**Gigablast**.com

**Ixquick**.com
**Dogpile**.com
**DuckDuckGo**.com
**Yippy**.com

## Other Resources

**How to use track changes from LinkedIn on YouTube:** https://www.youtube.com/watch?v=5_knruAysnA&t
**Grammar Girl, Mignon Fogarty, over at QuickandDirty-Tips:** http://www.quickanddirtytips.com/
**Scribophile "The Show and Tell Debate:"** http://www.scribophile.com/academy/the-show-versus-tell-debate
**OneLook Reverse Dictionary:** http://www.onelook.com/reverse-dictionary.shtml

# About the Author

**D**ebra L. Butterfield dreamed of being a writer since she was a pre-teen. Fulfillment of that dream began when she was forty-five years old and Focus on the Family hired her as a junior copywriter. In 2006, she stepped into the world of freelance writer. In 2014, she joined CrossRiver Media Group as an editor, and is now their editorial director.

She is passionate about helping other writers in their journey to publication. She blogs about writing at TheMotivationalEditor.com and does freelance editing in addition to her work with CrossRiver. She especially enjoys teaching workshops at writers conferences throughout the US.

Debra is the author of eight books including *Claiming Her Inheritance*, *Unshakable Faith*, and *Carried by Grace: A Guide for Mothers of Victims of Sexual Abuse*. She has contributed

stories to numerous anthologies and her article credits include CBN.com, *Susie, Live, The Vision, On Course* online, writers newsletters, and guest blogs.

Debra is a US Marine Corps veteran, enjoys the outdoors and, oddly enough, likes the smell of skunks. Her kids tell her take a deep breath whenever they smell one. Like most writers, she loves to read, usually not one book at a time either. She has lived as far west as Hawaii, as far east as Germany, and lots of places in between. Now living in Missouri, Debra has three adult children and two grandchildren.

To learn more, visit TheMotivationalEditor.com where you can subscribe to her blog. You'll find posts on a wide variety of writing-related topics designed to teach you the craft of writing, how to submit your manuscript, and how to market your book. You'll also find motivation and encouragement to help you persevere. (P.S. You'll get the terrific free download as well.) You'll receive an email whenever a new blog is posted and can find out where Debra is speaking.

### Other Books by Debra L. Butterfield
### Fiction

*Claiming Her Inheritance*
*Discovering Her Inheritance* (coming soon)
*Mystery on Maple Hill* (a short story ebook)

### Nonfiction

*Unshakable Faith: Living Strong in the Kingdom of God*
*Carried by Grace: a Guide for Mothers of Victims of Sexual Abuse*
*Abba's Promise: 33 Stories of God's Pledge to Provide*
*Abba's Answers: 30 Stories of God's Answers to Prayer*